Noah's Ark

A biblical and scientific look at the Genesis account

A POCKET GUIDE TO . . .

Noah's Ark

A biblical and scientific look at the the Genesis account

Petersburg, Kentucky, US

Reprinted July 2020

ISBN: 978-1-62691-632-6

Printed in China

AnswersInGenesis.org

Table of Contents

Introduction

The idea of a man building a giant boat to rescue humanity has been the subject of much interest throughout human history. From Ark-themed bathrooms and nursery accessories to irreverent portrayals in modern films, Noah and his Ark have been represented in many different ways. The Ark is a common target for those who wish to mock the Bible or turn its historical accounts into fables with an element of moral teaching. Rather than taking the account in the Bible at face value, many allow a modern "scientific" mind-set to impact their understanding of Scripture.

But what did the Ark really look like? Does the Bible shed any light on the size or construction of the Ark? How does the Ark compare to the ships we have today? How did Noah round up all of the animals on the earth? Has Noah's Ark been found? Is there any symbolism in the Ark? All of these questions, and more, will be answered as you explore this book.

When you look to Scripture as the authoritative writing that it is, you would expect what you see in the world around you to confirm those truths. An understanding of the size and proportions of the Ark, and the biblical classification of the created kinds, are supported by what we observe in nature. When we look at the evidence through the lens of Scripture, what we see in the world supports the factual nature of the account of Noah and the Ark as recorded.

Was There Really a Noah's Ark?

by Ken Ham and Tim Lovett

The account of Noah and the Ark is one of the most widely known events in the history of mankind. Unfortunately, like other Bible accounts, it is often taken as a mere fairy tale.

The Bible, though, is the true history book of the universe, and in that light, the most-asked questions about the Ark and Flood of Noah can be answered with authority and confidence.

How large was Noah's Ark?

> The length of the ark shall be three hundred cubits, its width fifty cubits, and its height thirty cubits. (Genesis 6:15)

Unlike many whimsical drawings that depict the Ark as some kind of overgrown houseboat (with giraffes sticking out the top), the Ark described in the Bible was a huge vessel. Not until the late 1800s was a ship built that exceeded the capacity of Noah's Ark.

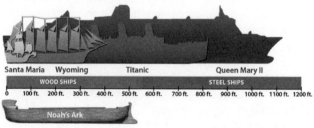

Santa Maria Wyoming Titanic Queen Mary II
WOOD SHIPS STEEL SHIPS
0 100 ft. 200 ft. 300 ft. 400 ft. 500 ft. 600 ft. 700 ft. 800 ft. 900 ft. 1000 ft. 1100 ft. 1200 ft.
Noah's Ark

The dimensions of the Ark are convincing for two reasons: the proportions are like that of a modern cargo ship, and it is about as large as a wooden ship can be built. The cubit gives us a good indication of size.[1] Using the most likely cubit length, an ancient royal cubit of at least 20.4 inches (0.518 m), we know that the Ark must have been no less than 510 feet (155 m) long, 85 feet (26 m) wide, and 51 feet (16 m) high. In the Western world, wooden sailing ships never got much longer than about 330 feet (100 m), yet the ancient Greeks built vessels at least this size 2,000 years earlier. China built huge wooden ships in the 1400s that may have been as large as the Ark. The biblical Ark is one of the largest wooden ships of all time—a mid-sized cargo ship by today's standards.

How could Noah build the Ark?

The Bible does not tell us that Noah and his sons built the Ark by themselves. Noah could have hired skilled laborers or had relatives, such as Methuselah and Lamech, help build the vessel. However, nothing indicates that they could not—or that they did not—build the Ark themselves in the time allotted. The physical strength and mental processes of men in Noah's day was at least as great (quite likely even superior) to our own.[2] They certainly would have had efficient means for harvesting and cutting timber, as well as for shaping, transporting, and erecting the massive beams and boards required.

If one or two men today can erect a large house in just 12 weeks, how much more could three or four men do in a few years? Adam's descendants were making complex musical instruments, forging metal, and building cities—their tools, machines, and techniques were not primitive.

History has shown that technology can be lost. In Egypt, China, and the Americas the earlier dynasties built more impressive buildings or had finer art or better science. Many so-called modern inventions turn out to be re-inventions, like concrete, which was used by the Romans.

Even accounting for the possible loss of technology due to the Flood, early post-Flood civilizations possessed all the engineering know-how necessary for a project like Noah's Ark. People were sawing and drilling wood in Noah's day, only a few centuries before the Egyptians were sawing and drilling granite; it is very reasonable! The idea that more primitive civilizations are further back in time is an evolutionary concept.

In reality, when God created Adam, he was perfect. Today, the individual human intellect has suffered from 6,000 years of sin and decay. The sudden rise in technology in the last few centuries has nothing to do with increasing intelligence; it is a combination of publishing and sharing ideas, and the spread of key inventions that became tools for investigation and manufacturing. One of the most recent tools is the computer, which compensates a great deal for our natural decline in mental performance and discipline, since it permits us to gather and store information as perhaps never before.

How could Noah round up so many animals?

Of the birds after their kind, of animals after their kind, and of every creeping thing of the earth after its kind, two of every kind will come to you, to keep them alive. (Genesis 6:20)

This verse tells us that Noah didn't have to search or travel to far-away places to bring the animals on board. The world map was completely different before the Flood, and on the basis of Genesis 1, there may have been only one continent. The animals simply arrived at the Ark as if called by a "homing instinct" (a behavior implanted in the animals by their Creator) and marched up the ramp, all by themselves.

Though this was probably a supernatural event (one that cannot be explained by our understanding of nature), compare it to the impressive migratory behavior we see in some animals today. We are still far from understanding all the marvelous animal behaviors exhibited in God's creation: the migration of Canada geese and other birds, the amazing flights of monarch butterflies, the annual travels of whales and fish, hibernation instincts, earthquake sensitivity, and countless other fascinating capabilities of God's animal kingdom.

Were dinosaurs on Noah's Ark?

The history of God's creation (told in Genesis 1 and 2) tells us that all the land-dwelling creatures were made on Day 6 of Creation Week—the same day God made Adam and Eve. Therefore, it is clear that dinosaurs (being land animals) were made with man.

Also, two of every kind (seven of some) of land animal boarded the Ark. Nothing indicates that any of the land animal kinds were already extinct before the Flood. Besides, the description of "behemoth" in chapter 40 of the book of Job (Job lived after the Flood) only fits with something like a sauropod dinosaur. The ancestor of "behemoth" must have been on board the Ark.[3]

We also find many dinosaurs that were trapped and fossilized in Flood sediment. Widespread legends of encounters with dragons give another indication that at least some dinosaurs survived the Flood. The only way this could happen is if they were on the Ark.

Juveniles of even the largest land animals do not present a size problem, and, being young, they have their full

Even the largest full-grown creatures were once small!

breeding life ahead of them. Yet most dinosaurs were not very large at all—some were the size of a chicken (although absolutely no relation to birds, as many evolutionists are now saying). Most scientists agree that the average size of a dinosaur is actually the size of a bison.

For example, God most likely brought Noah two young adult sauropods (e.g., apatosaurs), rather than two full-grown sauropods. The same goes for the elephant kind, the giraffe kind, and other animals that grow to be very large. However, there was adequate room for most fully grown adult animals anyway.

As far as the number of different types of dinosaurs, it should be recognized that, although there are hundreds of names for different varieties (species) of dinosaurs that have been discovered, there are probably only 60 to 80 actual different kinds.

How could a flood destroy every living thing?

And all flesh died that moved on the earth: birds and cattle and beasts and every creeping thing that creeps on the earth, and every man. All in whose nostrils was the breath of the spirit of life, all that was on the dry land, died. (Genesis 7:21–22)

Noah's Flood was much more destructive than any 40-day rainstorm ever could be. Scripture says that the "fountains of the great deep" broke open. In other words, earthquakes, volcanoes, and geysers of molten lava and scalding water were squeezed out of the earth's crust in a violent, explosive upheaval. These fountains were not stopped until 150 days into the Flood—so the earth was literally churning underneath the waters for about five months! The duration of the Flood was extensive, and Noah and his family were aboard the Ark for around a year.

Relatively recent local floods, volcanoes, and earth-quakes—though clearly devastating to life and land—are tiny in comparison to the worldwide catastrophe that destroyed "the world that then existed" (2 Peter 3:6). All land animals and people not on board the Ark were destroyed in the flood-waters—billions of animals were preserved in the great fossil record we see today.

How could the Ark survive the Flood?

The description of the Ark is very brief—Genesis 6:14–16. Those three verses contain critical information including overall dimensions, but Noah was almost certainly given more detail than this. Other divinely specified constructions in the Bible are meticulously detailed, like the descriptions of Moses' Tabernacle or the temple in Ezekiel's vision.

The Bible does not say the Ark was a rectangular box. In fact, Scripture gives no clue about the shape of Noah's Ark other than the proportions—length, width, and depth. Ships have long been described like this without ever implying a block-shaped hull.

Moses used the obscure term *tebah*, a word that is only used again for the basket that carried baby Moses (Exodus 2:3). One was a huge wooden ship and the other a tiny wicker basket. Both float, both rescue life, and both are covered. But the similarity ends there. We can be quite sure that the baby basket did not have the same proportions as the Ark, and Egyptian baskets of the time were typically rounded. Perhaps tebah means "lifeboat."

For many years biblical creationists have simply depicted the Ark as a rectangular box. This shape helped illustrate its size while avoiding the distractions of hull curvature. It also made it easy to compare volume. By using a short cubit and the maximum number of animal "kinds," creationists, as we've seen, have demonstrated how easily the Ark could fit the payload.[4] At the time, space was the main issue; other factors were secondary.

However, the next phase of research investigated sea-keeping (behavior and comfort at sea), hull strength, and stability. This began with a Korean study performed at the world-class ship research center (KRISO) in 1992.[5] The team of nine KRISO researchers was led by Dr. Hong, who is now director-general of the research center.

The study confirmed that the Ark could handle waves as high as 98 feet (30 m), and that the proportions of the biblical Ark are near optimal—an interesting admission from Dr. Hong, who believed evolutionary ideas. The study combined analysis, model wave testing, and ship standards, yet the concept was simple: compare the biblical Ark with 12 other vessels of the same volume but modified in length, width, or depth. Three qualities were measured—stability, hull strength, and comfort.

Ship qualities measured in the 1992 Korean study

While Noah's Ark was an average performer in each quality, it was among the best designs overall. In other words, the proportions show a careful design balance that is easily lost when proportions are modified the wrong way. It is no surprise that modern ships have similar proportions—those proportions work.

Interesting to note is the fact that this study makes nonsense of the claim that Genesis was written only a few centuries before Christ and was based on flood legends such as the Epic of Gilgamesh.[6] The Babylonian ark is a cube shape, something so far from reality that even the shortest hull in the Korean study was not even close. But we would expect mistakes from other flood accounts, like that of Gilgamesh, as the account of Noah would have been distorted as it was passed down through different cultures.

Yet one mystery remained. The Korean study did not hide the fact that some shorter hulls slightly outperformed the biblical Noah's Ark. Further work by Tim Lovett, one author of this chapter, and two naval architects, Jim King and Dr. Allen Magnuson, focused attention on the issue of broaching—being turned sideways by the waves.

How do we know what the waves were like? If there were no waves at all, stability, comfort, or strength would be unimportant, and the proportions would not matter. A shorter hull would then be a more efficient volume, taking less wood and less work. However, we can take clues from the proportions of the Ark itself. The Korean study had assumed waves came from every direction, giving shorter hulls an advantage. But real ocean waves usually have a dominant direction due to the wind, favoring a short, wide hull even more.

Another type of wave may also have affected the Ark during the Flood—tsunamis. Earthquakes can create tsunamis that devastate coastlines. However, when a tsunami travels in deep water it is imperceptible to a ship. During the Flood, the water would have been very deep—there is enough water in today's oceans to cover the earth to a depth of about 1.7 miles (2.7 km). The Bible states that the Ark rose "high above the earth" (Genesis 7:17). Launched from high ground by the rising floodwaters, the Ark would have avoided the initial devastation of coastlines and low-lying areas, and remained safe from tsunamis throughout the voyage.

After several months at sea, God sent a wind (Genesis 8:1), which could have produced very large waves since these waves can be produced by a strong, steady wind. Open-water testing confirms that any drifting vessel will naturally turn side-on to the waves (broach). With waves approaching the side of the vessel (beam sea), a long vessel like the Ark would be trapped in an uncomfortable situation; in heavy weather it could become dangerous. This could be overcome, however, by the vessel catching the wind (Genesis 8:1) at the bow and catching the water at the stern—aligning itself like a wind vane. These features appear to have inspired a number of ancient ship designs. Once the Ark points into the waves, the long, ship-like proportions create a more comfortable and controlled voyage. Traveling slowly with the wind, it had no need for speed, but the Bible does say the Ark moved about on the surface of the waters (Genesis 7:18).

However, not all waves are aligned with the local wind, the ark may also encounter distant swells from any direction. The first line of defense comes from the excellent proportions of the ark, confirmed in a study by a world-class ship research center in Korea. In addition, the outer keels that provide protection on land also improve roll damping in the waves, much like the bilge keels of a modern ship. So it is prudent for Noah to put lots of ancient ingenuity into the project of his life.

Compared to a ship-like bow and stern, blunt ends are not as strong, have edges that are vulnerable to damage during launch and beaching, and give a rougher ride. Since the Bible gives proportions like that of a true ship, it makes sense that it should look and act ship-like. The below design is an attempt to flesh out the biblical outline using real-life experiments and archeological evidence of ancient ships.

Central (noon positioned) skylight with 1 cubit high combing

Wind catching rigid fin and deckhouse

Skeg extends beyond stern, a "mystery" of ancient ships.

Wind

While Scripture does not point out a wind-catching feature at the bow, the abbreviated account we are given in Genesis makes no mention of drinking water, the number of animals, or the way they got out of the Ark either.

Nothing in this newly depicted Ark contradicts Scripture; in fact, it shows how accurate Scripture is, since the proportions are so realistic! (For more information on the design of the Ark, see chapter 3, "Thinking Outside the Box.")

Where did all the water go?

And the waters receded continually from the earth. At the end of the hundred and fifty days the waters decreased. (Genesis 8:3)

Simply put, the water from the Flood is in the oceans and seas we see today. Three-quarters of the earth's surface is covered with water.

As even secular geologists observe, it does appear that the continents were at one time "together" and not separated by the vast oceans of today. The forces involved in the Flood were certainly sufficient to change all of this.

Scripture indicates that God formed the ocean basins, raising the land out of the water, so that the floodwaters returned to a safe place. (Some theologians believe Psalm 104:7–9 may refer to this event.) Some creation scientists believe this breakup of the continent was part of the mechanism that ultimately caused the Flood.[7]

Some have speculated, because of Genesis 10:25, that the continental break occurred during the time of Peleg. However, this division is mentioned in the context of the Tower of Babel's language division of the whole earth (Genesis 10–11). So the context points to a dividing of the languages and people groups, not the land breaking apart.

If there were a massive movement of continents during the time of Peleg, there would have been another worldwide flood. The Bible indicates that the mountains of Ararat existed for the Ark to land in them (Genesis 8:4); so the Indian-Australian Plate and Eurasian Plate had to have already collided, indicating that the continents had already shifted prior to Peleg.

Was Noah's Flood global?

> And the waters prevailed exceedingly on the earth, and all the high hills under the whole heaven were covered. The waters prevailed fifteen cubits upward, and the mountains were covered. (Genesis 7:19–20)

Many Christians today claim that the Flood of Noah's time was only a local flood. These people generally believe in a local flood because they have accepted the widely believed evolutionary history of the earth, which interprets fossil layers as the history of the sequential appearance of life over millions of years.[8]

Scientists once understood the fossils, which are buried in water-carried sediments of mud and sand, to be mostly the result of the great Flood. Those who now accept millions of years of gradual accumulation of fossils have, in their way of thinking, explained away the evidence for the global Flood. Hence, many compromising Christians insist on a local flood.

Secularists deny the possibility of a worldwide Flood at all. If they would think from a biblical perspective, however, they would see the abundant evidence for the global Flood. As someone once quipped, "I wouldn't have seen it if I hadn't believed it."

Those who accept the evolutionary timeframe, with its fossil accumulation, also rob the Fall of Adam of its serious consequences. They put the fossils, which testify of disease, suffering, and death, before Adam and Eve sinned and brought death and suffering into the world. In doing this, they also undermine the meaning of the death and resurrection of

A local flood that rose above the mountains?

Christ. Such a scenario also robs all meaning from God's description of His finished creation as "very good."

If the Flood only affected the area of Mesopotamia, as some claim, why did Noah have to build an Ark? He could have walked to the other side of the mountains and escaped. Most importantly, if the Flood were local, people not living in the vicinity of the Flood would not have been affected by it. They would have escaped God's judgment on sin.

In addition, Jesus believed that the Flood killed every person not on the Ark. What else could Christ mean when He likened the coming world judgment to the judgment of "all" men in the days of Noah (Matthew 24:37–39)?

In 2 Peter 3, the coming judgment by fire is likened to the former judgment by water in Noah's Flood. A partial judgment in Noah's day, therefore, would mean a partial judgment to come.

If the Flood were only local, how could the waters rise to 20 feet (6 m) above the mountains (Genesis 7:20)? Water seeks its own level; it could not rise to cover the local mountains while leaving the rest of the world untouched.

Even what is now Mt. Everest was once covered with water and uplifted afterward.[9] If we even out the ocean basins and flatten out the mountains, there is enough water to cover the entire earth by about 1.7 miles (2.7 km).[10] Also important to note is that, with the leveling out of the oceans and mountains, the Ark would not have been riding at the height of the current Mt. Everest, thus no need for such things as oxygen masks either.

There's more. If the Flood were a local flood, God would have repeatedly broken His promise never to send such a flood again. God put a rainbow in the sky as a covenant between God and man and the animals that He would never repeat such an event. There have been huge local floods in recent times (e.g., in Bangladesh, Indonesia, and Japan); but never has there been another global Flood that killed all life on the land.

Where is the evidence in the earth for Noah's Flood?

For this they willingly forget: that by the word of God the heavens were of old, and the earth standing out of water and in the water, by which the world that then existed perished, being flooded with water. (2 Peter 3:5–6)

Evidence of Noah's Flood can be seen all over the earth, from seabeds to mountaintops. Whether you travel by car, train, or plane, the physical features of the earth's terrain clearly indicate a catastrophic past, from canyons and craters to coal beds and caverns. Some layers of strata extend across continents, revealing the effects of a huge catastrophe.

The earth's crust has massive amounts of layered sedimentary rock, sometimes miles (kilometers) deep! These layers of sand, soil, and material—mostly laid down by water—were once soft like mud, but they are now hard stone.

Encased in these sedimentary layers are billions of dead things (fossils of plants and animals) buried very quickly. The evidence all over the earth is staring everyone in the face.

Where is Noah's Ark today?

The Ark landed in mountains. The ancient name for these mountains could refer to several areas in the Middle East, such as Mt. Ararat in Turkey or other mountain ranges in neighboring countries.

Mt. Ararat has attracted the most attention because it has permanent ice, and some people report to have seen the Ark. Many expeditions have searched for the Ark there. There is no conclusive evidence of the Ark's location or survival; after all, it landed on the mountains about 4,500 years ago. Also it could easily have deteriorated, been destroyed, or been used as lumber by Noah and his descendants.

Some scientists and Bible scholars, though, believe the Ark could indeed be preserved—perhaps to be providentially revealed at a future time as a reminder of the past judgment and the judgment to come, although the same could be said for things like the Ark of the Covenant or other biblical icons. Jesus said, "If they do not hear Moses and the prophets, neither will they be persuaded though one rise from the dead" (Luke 16:31).

The Ark is unlikely to have survived without supernatural intervention, but this is neither promised nor expected from Scripture. However, it is a good idea to check if it still exists. (For more information on the search for Noah's Ark, see page 71, "Has Noah's Ark Been Found?").

Why did God destroy the earth that He had made?

Then the Lord saw that the wickedness of man was great in the earth, and that every intent of the thoughts of his heart was only evil continually. But Noah found grace in the eyes of the Lord. (Genesis 6:5, 6:8)

These verses speak for themselves. Every human being on the face of the earth had turned after the wickedness in their own hearts, but Noah, because of his righteousness before God, was spared from God's judgment, along with his wife, their sons, and their wives. As a result of man's wickedness, God sent judgment on all mankind. As harsh as the destruction was, no living person was without excuse.

God also used the Flood to separate and to purify those who believed in Him from those who didn't. Throughout history and throughout the Bible, this cycle has taken place time after time: separation, purification, judgment, and redemption.

Without God and without a true knowledge and understanding of Scripture, which provides the true history of the world, man is doomed to repeat the same mistakes over and over again.

How is Christ like the Ark?

For the Son of Man has come to save that which was lost. (Matthew 18:11)

As God's Son, the Lord Jesus Christ is like Noah's Ark. Jesus came to seek and to save the lost. Just as Noah and his family were saved by the Ark, rescued by God from the floodwaters, so anyone who believes in Jesus as Lord and Savior will be spared from the coming final judgment of mankind, rescued by God from the fire that will destroy the earth after the last days (2 Peter 3:7).

Noah and his family had to go through a doorway into the Ark to be saved, and the Lord shut the door behind them (Genesis 7:16). So we too have to go through a "doorway" to be saved so that we won't be eternally separated from God. The Son of God, Jesus, stepped into history to pay the penalty for our sin of rebellion. Jesus said, "I am the door. If anyone enters by Me, he will be saved, and will go in and out and find pasture" (John 10:9).

1. The cubit was defined as the length of the forearm from elbow to fingertip. Ancient cubits vary anywhere from 17.5 inches (45 cm) to 22 inches (56 cm), the longer sizes dominating the major ancient constructions. Despite this, even a conservative 18 inch (46 cm) cubit describes a sizeable vessel.

2. For the evidence, see Donald Chittick, *The Puzzle of Ancient Man* (Newberg, OR: Creation Compass, 1998) and Don Landis, Ed., *The Genius of Ancient Man* (Green Forest, AR: Master Books, 2012). These books detail evidence of man's intelligence in early post-Flood civilizations.

3. For some remarkable evidence that dinosaurs have lived until relatively recent times, see chapter 12 of *The New Answers Book 1* (Green Forest, AR: Master Books, 2006). Also read Ken Ham, *The Great Dinosaur Mystery Solved* (Green Forest, AR: Master Books, 2000). Also visit answersingenesis. org/go/dinosaurs.

4. To read a thorough study on this research, see *Noah's Ark: A Feasibility Study* by John Woodmorappe (see Ref. 4)

5. Seok Won Hong et al., "Safety Investigation of Noah's Ark in a Seaway," *TJ* 8 no. 1 (1994): 26–36, answersingenesis.org/tj/v8/i1/noah.asp.

6. For deeper study on this, please see Nozomi Osanai, "A Comparison of Scientific Reliability, A comparative study of the flood accounts in the Gilgamesh Epic and Genesis," Answers in Genesis, answersingenesis.org/go/gilgamesh.

7. See chapter 14 by Dr. Andrew Snelling in *The New Answers Book 1* (Green Forest, AR: Master Books, 2006).

8. For compelling evidence that the earth is not billions of years old, read *The Young Earth* by Dr. John Morris and *Thousands . . . not Billions* by Dr. Don DeYoung; also see answersingenesis.org/go/young.

9. Mount Everest is more than 5 miles (8 km) high. How, then, could the Flood have covered "all the mountains under the whole heaven?" Before the Flood, the mountains were not so high. The mountains today were formed only toward the end of, and after, the Flood by collision of the tectonic plates and the associated up-thrusting. In support of this, the layers that form the uppermost parts of Mt. Everest are themselves composed of fossil-bearing, water-deposited layers.

10. A.R. Wallace, *Man's Place in the Universe* (New York: McClure, Phillips & Co, 1903), pp. 225–226; wku.edu/~smithch/wallace/S728-3.htm.

Ken Ham is President and CEO of Answers in Genesis–US, the Creation Museum, and Ark Encounter. Ken's bachelor's degree in applied science (with an emphasis on environmental biology) was awarded by the Queensland Institute of Technology in Australia. He also holds a diploma of education from the University of Queensland. In recognition of the contribution Ken has made to the church in the US and internationally, Ken has been awarded two honorary doctorates: a Doctor of Divinity (1997) from Temple Baptist College in Cincinnati, Ohio, and a Doctor of Literature (2004) from Liberty University in Lynchburg, Virginia.

Ken has authored or co-authored many books concerning the authority and accuracy of God's Word and the effects of evolutionary thinking, including his best seller, *The Lie: Evolution*.

Since moving to America in 1987, Ken has become one of the most in-demand Christian conference speakers and talk show guests in America. He has appeared on national shows such as Fox's *The O'Reilly Factor* and *Fox and Friends in the Morning*; CNN's *The Situation Room with Wolf Blitzer*, ABC's *Good Morning America*, the BBC, *CBS News Sunday Morning*, *The NBC Nightly News with Brian Williams*, and *The PBS News Hour with Jim Lehrer*.

Tim Lovett earned his degree in mechanical engineering from Sydney University (Australia) and was an instructor for 12 years in technical college engineering courses. Tim has studied the Flood and the Ark for 13 years and is widely recognized for his cutting-edge research on the design and structure of Noah's Ark. He helped design Noah's Ark at the Ark Encounter in Williamstown, Kentucky.

Flood Legends: A World of Stories Based on Truth

by A. J. Monty White

There are hundreds of stories and legends about a world-wide flood. Why do diverse cultures share a strikingly similar story?

Did you know that stories about a worldwide flood are found in historic records all over the world? According to Dr. Duane Gish in his popular book *Dinosaurs by Design*, there are more than 270 such stories, most of which share a common theme and similar characters. So many flood stories with such similarities surely come from the Flood of Noah's day.

A historical event

The worldwide catastrophic Flood, recorded in the book of Genesis, was a real event that affected real people. In fact, those people carried the knowledge of this event with them when they spread to the ends of the earth.

The Bible declares that the earth-covering cataclysm of Noah's day is an obvious fact of history. People "willfully forget: that . . . the world that then existed perished, being flooded with water" (2 Peter 3:5–6). This Flood left many evidences, from the fact that over 70% of the rocks on continents were laid down by water and contain fossils, to the widespread flood legends. Both of these evidences provide compelling support for this historical event.

If only eight people—Noah's family—survived the Flood, we would expect there to be historical evidence of a worldwide flood. If you think about it, the evidence would be historical records in the nations of the world, and this is what we have, as the chart [at right] indicates. Stories of the Flood—distorted though they may be—exist in practically all nations, from ancient Babylon onward. This evidence must not be lightly dismissed. If there never was a world-wide Flood, then why are there so many stories about it?

From generation to generation

The reason for these flood stories is not difficult to understand. When we turn to the history book of the universe, the Bible, we learn that Noah's descendants stayed together for approximately 100 years, until God confused their languages at Babel (Genesis 11:1–9). As these people moved away from Babel, their descendants formed nations based primarily on the languages they shared in common. Through those languages, the story of the Flood was shared, until it became embedded in their cultural history.

Similar stories

Hawaiians have a flood story that tells of a time when, long after the death of the first man, the world became a wicked, terrible place. Only one good man was left, and his name was Nu-u. He made a great canoe with a house on it and filled it with animals. In this story, the waters came up over all the earth and killed all the people; only Nu-u and his family were saved.

Another flood story is from China. It records that Fuhi, his wife, three sons, and three daughters escaped a great flood and were the only people alive on earth. After the great flood, they repopulated the world.

As the story of the Flood was verbally passed from one generation to the next, some aspects would have been lost or altered. And this is what has happened, as we can see from the chart. However, as seen in the given examples, each story shares remarkable similarities to the account of Noah in the

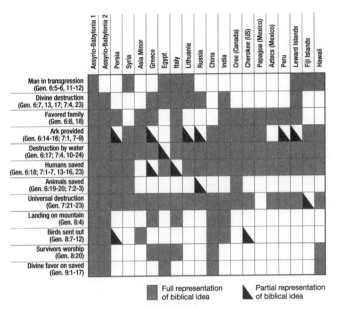

Global flood traditions

This chart shows the similarities that several myths have with the Genesis account of Noah's Flood. Although there are varying degrees of accuracy, these legends and stories all contain similarities to aspects of the same historical event—Noah's Flood.

Chart adapted from B.C. Nelson, *The Deluge Story in Stone*, Appendix 11: Flood Traditions, Figure 38 (Minneapolis, Minnesota: Augsburg, 1931).

Bible. This is true even in some of the details, such as the name Nu-u in the Hawaiian flood story. "Nu-u" is very similar to "Noah."

What these stories mean

God clearly sent a worldwide Flood to punish humankind for their evil and corrupt ways (Genesis 6:5, 6:11). Even though Flood-affirming evidence from geology and other areas of study is abundant, we don't need this evidence to know what happened. Starting with the Bible and the history that God faithfully recorded there, Christians have a tool to interpret the evidence that evolutionists and non-Christians do not. We have the record of what happened, from the one who was there.

Monty White earned his BSc degree in chemistry and his PhD in gas kinetics from the University of Wales, Aberystwyth. Dr. White is the former CEO of Answers in Genesis-UK/Europe and has traveled extensively throughout Europe lecturing on creationists' views of origins.

Thinking Outside the Box

by Tim Lovett

While the Bible gives us essential details on many things, including the size and proportions of Noah's Ark, it does not necessarily specify the precise shape of this vessel. It is important to understand, however, that this lack of physical description is consistent with other historical accounts in Scripture.[1] So how should we illustrate what the Ark looked like? The two main options include a default rectangular shape reflecting the lack of specific detail, and a more fleshed-out design that incorporates principles of ship design from maritime science, while remaining consistent with the Bible's size and proportions.

Genesis describes the Ark in three verses, which require careful examination:

6:14—"Make yourself an ark [*tebah*] of gopher wood; make rooms [*qinniym*] in the ark, and cover it inside and outside with pitch [*kofer*].

6:15—"And this is how you shall make it: The length of the ark shall be three hundred cubits, its width fifty cubits, and its height thirty cubits.

6:16—"You shall make a window [*tsohar*] for the ark, and you shall finish it to a cubit from above; and set the door of the ark in its side. You shall make it with lower, second, and third decks."

Most Bibles make some unusual translation choices for certain key words. Elsewhere in the Bible the Hebrew word translated here as "rooms" is usually rendered "nests"; "pitch" would normally be called "covering"; and "window" would be "noon light." Using these more typical meanings, the Ark would be something like this:

The *tebah* (Ark) was made from gopher wood, it had nests inside, and it was covered with a pitch-like substance inside and out. It was 300 cubits long, 50 cubits wide, and 30 cubits high. It had a noon light that ended a cubit upward and above, it had a door in the side, and there were three decks.

As divine specifications go, Moses offered more elaborate details about the construction of the Tabernacle, which suggests this might be the abridged version of Noah's complete directions. On the other hand, consider how wise Noah must have been after having lived several centuries. The instructions that we have recorded in Genesis may be all he needed to be told. But in any case, 300 cubits is a big ship, not some whimsical houseboat with giraffe necks sticking out the top.

Scripture gives no clue about the shape of Noah's Ark beyond its proportions—length, breadth, and depth. Ships have long been described like this without ever implying a block-shaped hull.

The scale of the Ark is huge yet remarkably realistic when compared to the largest wooden ships in history. The proportions are even more amazing—they are just like a modern cargo ship.

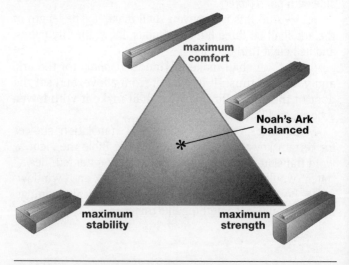

maximum comfort

Noah's Ark balanced

maximum stability

maximum strength

Scientific study endorses seaworthiness of Ark

Noah's Ark was the focus of a major 1992 scientific study headed by Dr. Seon Hong at the world-class ship research center KRISO, based in Daejeon, South Korea. Dr. Hong's team compared twelve hulls of different proportions to discover which design was most practical. No hull shape was found to significantly outperform the 4,300-year-old biblical design. In fact, the Ark's careful balance is easily lost if the proportions are modified, rendering the vessel either unstable, prone to fracture, or dangerously uncomfortable.

The research team found that the proportions of Noah's Ark carefully balanced the conflicting demands of stability (resistance to capsizing), comfort (seakeeping), and strength. In fact, the Ark has the same proportions as a modern cargo ship.

The study also confirmed that the Ark could handle waves as high as 100 feet (30 m). Dr. Hong is now director general of the facility and claims "life came from the sea," clearly not the words of a creationist on a mission to promote the worldwide Flood. Endorsing the seaworthiness of Noah's Ark obviously did not damage Dr. Hong's credibility.

Dr. Seon Won Hong was principal research scientist when he headed up the Noah's Ark investigation. In May 2005 Dr. Hong was appointed director general of MOERI (formerly KRISO). Dr. Hong earned a BS degree in naval architecture from Seoul National University and a PhD degree in applied mechanics from the University of Michigan, Ann Arbor.

All this makes nonsense of the claim that Genesis was written only a few centuries before Christ, as a mere retelling of earlier Babylonian flood legends such as the *Epic of Gilgamesh*. The *Epic of Gilgamesh* story describes a cube-shaped ark, which would have given a dangerously rough ride. This is neither accurate nor scientific. Noah's Ark is the original, while the Gilgamesh Epic is a later distortion.

What about the shape?

For many years biblical creationists have simply depicted the Ark as a rectangular box. This helped emphasize its size. It was easy to explain capacity and illustrate how easily the Ark could have handled the payload. With the rectangular shape, the Ark's stability against rolling could even be demonstrated by simple calculations.

Yet the Bible does not say the Ark must be a rectangular box. In fact, Scripture does not elaborate about the shape of Noah's Ark beyond those superb, overall proportions—length, breadth, and depth. Ships have long been described like this without implying a block-shaped hull.

In Hebrew "Ark" is the obscure term *tebah*, a word that appears only one other time when it describes the basket that carried baby Moses (Exodus 2:3). One was a huge, wooden ship and the other a tiny, wicker basket. Both floated, both preserved life, and both were covered; but the similarity ends there. If the word implied anything about shape, it would be "an Egyptian basket-like shape," typically rounded. More likely, however, *tebah* means something else, like "lifeboat."[2]

The Bible leaves the details regarding the shape of the Ark wide open—anything from a rectangular box with hard right angles and no curvature at all, to a ship-like form. Box-like has the largest carrying capacity, but a ship-like design would be safer and more comfortable in heavy seas. Such discussion is irrelevant if God intended to sustain the Ark no matter how well designed and executed.

Clues from the Bible

Some question whether the Ark was actually built to handle rough seas, but the Bible gives some clues about the sea conditions during the Flood:

- The Ark had the proportions of a seagoing vessel built for waves (Genesis 6:15).

- Logically, a mountain-covering, global Flood would not be dead calm (Genesis 7:19).

- The Ark moved about on the surface of the waters (Genesis 7:18).

- God made a wind to pass over the earth (Genesis 8:1).
- The Hebrew word for the Flood (*mabbul*) could imply being carried along.

The 1993 Korean study showed that some shorter hulls slightly outperformed the Ark model with biblical proportions. The study assumed waves came from every direction, favoring shorter hulls like that of a modern lifeboat. So why was Noah's Ark so long if it didn't need to be streamlined for moving through the water?

The answer lies in ride comfort (seakeeping). This requires a longer hull, at the cost of strength and stability, not to mention more wood. The Ark's high priority for comfort suggests that the anticipated waves must have been substantial.

Designed for tsunamis

Was the Ark designed for tsunamis? Not really. Tsunamis devastate coastlines, but when a tsunami travels in deep water, it is almost imperceptible to a ship. During the Flood, the water was probably very deep—there is enough water in today's oceans to cover a relatively flat earth to a consistent depth of over 2 miles (3.2 km). The Bible states that the Ark rose "high above the earth" (Genesis 7:17) and was stranded early (Genesis 8:4), before mountaintops were seen. If the launch was a mirror of the landing—the Ark being the last thing to float—it would have been a deep-water voyage from start to finish.

The worst waves may have been caused by wind, just like today. After several months at sea, God made a wind to pass over the earth. This suggests a large-scale weather pattern likely to produce waves with a dominant direction. It is an established fact that such waves would cause any drifting vessel to be driven sideways (broaching). A long vessel like the Ark would remain locked in this sideways position, an uncomfortable and even dangerous situation in heavy weather.

However, broaching can be avoided if the vessel catches the wind at one end and is "rooted" in the water at the other—turning like a weather vane into the wind. Once the Ark points into the waves, the long proportions create a more comfortable and controlled voyage. It had no need for speed, but the Ark did "move about on the surface of the waters."

The box-like Ark is not entirely disqualified as a safe option, but sharp edges are more vulnerable to damage during launch and landing. Blunt ends would also produce a rougher ride and allow the vessel to be more easily thrown around (but, of course, God could have miraculously kept the ship's precious cargo safe, regardless of the comfort factor). Since the Bible gives proportions consistent with those of a true cargo ship, it makes sense that it should look and act like a ship, too.

Coincidentally, certain aspects of this design appear in some of the earliest large ships depicted in pottery from Mesopotamia, which is not long after the Flood. It makes sense that shipwrights, who are conservative as a rule, would continue to include elements of the only ship to survive the global Flood—Noah's Ark.

Scripture does not record direction-keeping features attached to the Ark. They might have been obvious to a 500-year-old, or perhaps they were common among ships in Noah's day as they were afterwards. At the same time, the brief specifications in Genesis make no mention of other important details, such as storage of drinking water, disposal of excrement, or the way to get out of the Ark. Obviously Noah needed to know how many animals were coming, but this is not recorded either.

The Bible gives clear instruction for the construction of a number of things, but it does not specify many aspects of the Ark's construction. Nothing in this newly depicted Ark contradicts Scripture, even though it may be different from more accepted designs. But this design, in fact, shows us just how reasonable Scripture is as it depicts a stable, comfortable, and seaworthy vessel that was capable of fulfilling all the requirements stated in Scripture.

Details of design

Scripture gives no clue about the details of Noah's Ark beyond its proportions that are given in Genesis 6:15, which reads: "And this is how you shall make it: The length of the ark shall be three hundred cubits, its width fifty cubits, and its height thirty cubits." This new design incorporates the following features that are found on ancient ocean-going vessels.

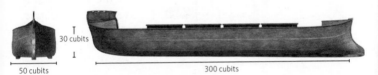

30 cubits

50 cubits

300 cubits

1. Something to catch the wind

Wind-driven waves would cause a drifting vessel to turn dangerously side-on to the weather. However, such waves could be safely navigated by making the Ark steer itself with a wind-catching obstruction on the bow. To be effective, this obstruction must be large enough to overcome the turning effect of the waves. While many designs could work, the possibility shown here reflects the high stems which were a hallmark of ancient ships.

2. A window

Any opening on the deck of a ship needs a wall (combing) to prevent water from flowing in, especially when the ship rolls. In this illustration, the window "ends a cubit upward and above," as described in Genesis 6:16. The central position of the skylight is chosen to reflect the idea of a "noon light." This also means that the window does not need to

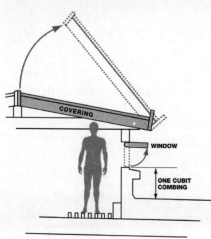

be exactly one cubit. Perhaps the skylight had a transparent roof (even more a "noon light"), or the skylight roof could be opened (which might correspond to when "Noah removed the covering of the Ark"). While variations are possible, a window without combing is not the most logical solution.

3. Mortise and tenon planking

Ancient shipbuilders usually began with a shell of planks (strakes) and then built internal framing (ribs) to fit inside. This is the complete reverse of the familiar European method where planking was added to the frame. In shell-first construction, the planks must be attached to each

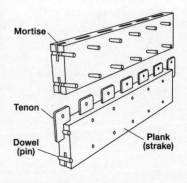

other somehow. Some used overlapping (clinker) planks that were dowelled or nailed, others used rope to sew the planks together. The ancient Greeks used a sophisticated system where the planks were interlocked with thousands of precise mortise and tenon joints. The resulting hull was strong enough to ram another ship, yet light enough to be hauled onto a beach by the crew. If this is what the Greeks could do centuries before Christ, what could Noah do centuries after Tubal-Cain invented forged metal tools?

4. Ramps

Ramps help to get animals and heavy loads between decks. Running them across the hull avoids cutting through important deck beams, and this location is away from the middle of the hull where bending stresses are highest. (This placement also better utilizes the irregular space at bow and stern.)

5. Something to catch the water

To assist in turning the Ark to point with the wind, the stern should resist being pushed sideways. This is the same as a fixed rudder or skeg that provides directional control. There are many ways this could be done, but here we are

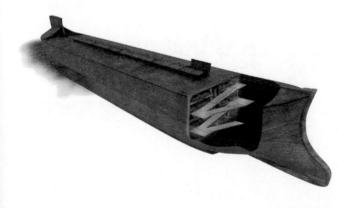

reflecting the "mysterious" stern extensions seen on the earliest large ships of the Mediterranean.

Was Noah's Ark the biggest ship ever built?

Few wooden ships have ever come close to the size of Noah's Ark. One possible challenge comes from the Chinese treasure ships of Yung He in the 1400s. An older contender is the ancient Greek trireme *Tessaronteres*.

At first historians dismissed ancient Greek claims that the *Tessaronteres* was 425 feet (130 m) long. But as more information was learned, the reputation of these early shipbuilders grew markedly. One of the greatest challenges to the construction of large wooden ships is finding a way to lay planks around the outside in a way that will ensure little or no leaking, which is caused when there is too much movement between the planks. Apparently, the Greeks had access to an extraordinary method of planking that was lost for centuries, and only recently brought to light by marine archaeology.

It is not known when or where this technique originated. Perhaps they used a method that began with the Ark. After all, if the Greeks could do it, why not Noah?

The Ark is near the maximum size that is known to be possible for a wooden vessel.

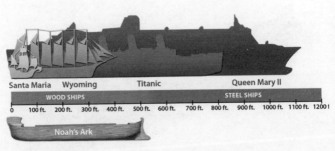

How big was the Ark? It depends on your cubit size! To get the 510 feet (155 m) given here, we used a cubit of 20.4 inches (51.8 cm). This diagram shows how Noah's Ark compares to other large ships.

1. Other objects spoken of in Scripture lack physical details which have been discovered (through archaeology and other research) later (e.g., the walls of Jericho were actually double and situated on a hillside—one higher than the other with a significant space of several feet between them).

2. C. Cohen, "Hebrew TBH: Proposed Etymologies," *The Journal of the Ancient Near Eastern Society (JANES)*, (1972): 36–51. (The journal was at that time called *The Journal of the Ancient Near Eastern Society of Columbia University*, Ancient Near Eastern Society of Columbia University, New York.)

Mything the Boat

by Dan Lietha

Noah's Ark is not just an old sea vessel floating alone in the pages of the Bible—it's a modern marketing extravaganza! Images of Noah's Ark—mostly directed at children—are everywhere: on fine art prints, children's books, wallpaper, toys, tapestries, greeting cards, T-shirts, magazine and TV ads, posters, wall decorations, and even business logos. And these images are not just aimed at the "religious" market; they are also hot items among the secular crowd.

Have you ever stopped to think how the Ark—such a powerful reminder of God's judgment—became so popular, considering the rejection of the true account of Noah's Flood by so many?

It can't be because of what the Ark really stands for. The Bible says that people are willingly ignorant that "the world that then was, being overflowed with water, perished" (2 Peter 3:5–6, KJV).

A clue to the Ark's popularity can be found in the Ark images themselves.

Redesigners of the lost Ark

Most Ark images bear little resemblance to the one described in Genesis. Artists generally ignore the information in Scripture in favor of a wide variety of imaginative shapes, sizes, and themes. The most common version is a toy-like boat, stuffed full of cuddly animals that crowd around Noah. Why is that?

Some artists treat the Ark like an amusing myth or children's fairy tale. They do not believe that the story is an account of actual events, and therefore they have no problem in doing anything they want with it.

Even artists and companies who believe the Bible's account of Noah's Flood sometimes choose to create a caricature of the Ark for artistic and sales reasons. For instance, small arks take less to time to draw, are cute, sell well, and make it easy to show the entire Ark and animals in one scene. And small arks aren't controversial, either, because they don't look real.

An Ark of biblical proportions

In addition to a lack of accuracy, the modern arks have a more serious drawback. One of the most-asked questions about Noah's Ark is how Noah fit all the animals into it. The size of the Ark is critical to the believability of the biblical account, and so is a realistic shape that could survive the Flood. Yet the Ark images that come to most people's minds fall far short.

In our modern, media-saturated culture, it is true that seeing is believing, especially for young children. Images make a strong impression and often overshadow the biblical account, even for those who have a moderate familiarity with whatever event is being described. So while airplanes and other well-known objects may be fine to caricature, promoting poor caricatures of the Ark can be harmful.

Sadly, with the best of intentions, the Church has promoted cutesy caricatures of the Ark in Sunday school materials and other literature, leaving the world largely unaware of the real message of the Ark that God instructed Noah to build.

The Bible explains why the modern world is willingly ignorant. It's because they don't want to face the reality that judgment is coming again: "But the heavens and the earth, which are now preserved by the same word, are reserved for fire until the day of judgment and perdition of ungodly men" (2 Peter 3:7).

CARTOONS—THEY CAN ACCURATELY DEPICT TRUTH

The cartoon ark (above) is an example of how Noah's Ark is commonly misrepresented. However, the problem does not lie in cartooning as a form of illustration, but rather the degree of distortion applied in the specific cartoon. For example, when the same distorted cartoon ark is depicted in a realistic setting (below, top), the picture remains an absurd portrayal of Noah's Ark. However, a cartoonist can draw the Ark in a way that reflects the true size and dimensions of the boat described in Genesis (below, bottom). Cartoons can be a very effective way to communicate accurate truth to all ages.

WE REALLY MISSED THE BOAT!

Dan Lietha, cartoonist and illustrator for AiG, graduated from the Joe Kubert School of Cartoon and Graphic Art. Some of his projects include *After Eden* and the *Creationwise* comic strip. He has also illustrated the book *When Dragons' Hearts Were Good* and the *Answers for Kids* curriculum.

How Could Eight People Care for the Animals on the Ark?

by Mike Belknap and Tim Chaffey

One of the most important issues relating to the Bible's Flood account is the topic of animals on the Ark. The estimated numbers, sizes, and types of Ark animals impacts nearly every aspect of the vessel's interior operations, including time and labor expenditures, food and water needs, space and waste management, and enclosure design.[1]

The subject of fitting and caring for all the required animals on the Ark is a significant point of contention between biblical creationists and skeptics. However, properly addressing these concerns is more complicated than a mere compilation of data about different animal species. First, we have to answer some fundamental questions.

Which animals were required on the Ark?

The Bible informs us that the Ark housed representatives of every land-dependent, air-breathing animal—ones that could not otherwise survive the Flood (Genesis 7:21–23). Conversely, Noah did not care for marine animals, and he probably did not need to bring insects, with the possible exception of delicate insects like butterflies and moths—since most insects could survive outside the Ark. Also, they take in oxygen through spiracles in their skin, and the Bible specifies that those creatures killed outside of the Ark were those "in whose nostrils was the breath of the spirit of life."

How many species are in the world today?

Skeptics often assert that there are millions of species in the world—far more than the number that could fit on the Ark. However, according to estimates published in 2014, there are fewer than 1.8 million documented species of organisms in the world. Consider also that over 98 percent of those species are fish, invertebrates, and non-animals (like plants and bacteria). This means that there are fewer than 34,000 species of known, land-dependent vertebrates in the world today.[2]

Species or kinds?

Though wild animals today are often considered according to their *species*, the Bible deals with animals according to their *min*—a common Hebrew word usually translated as "kind." We can infer from Scripture that God created plants and animals to reproduce after their kinds (Genesis 1:11–25), and it is clear from various texts that a kind is often a broader category than the current concept of a species. This means that a kind may contain many different species. Since Noah was only sent select representatives from relevant kinds, all land-dwelling vertebrate species not present on the Ark were wiped out. Therefore, if we see an Ark kind represented today by different species—e.g., horses, zebras, and donkeys of the equid kind—those species have developed *since* the time of the Flood. Therefore, species are simply varying expressions of a particular kind.

What is an animal kind?

There are numerous approaches to defining a kind, but one of the simplest is *a created distinct type of organism and all of the related descendants*. Kinds are often referred to as baramins (from the Hebrew words for "created" and "kind"), and the study of created kinds is called baraminology.

What are the criteria for identifying kinds?

In 2011, Ark Encounter researchers began in-depth animal studies with the goal of identifying the maximum number of Ark kinds. The researchers applied three primary criteria in estimating the Ark kinds: hybridization, cognitum, and statistical baraminology.[3]

Hybrid data is the most favored method in identifying kinds. Researchers believe that only closely related animals can successfully produce offspring, and this is consistent with the Bible's emphasis on the relationship between reproduction and created kinds. Since only animals in the same kind are related, hybrids positively identify which animals are part of the same kind. The usefulness of hybrid data is limited, however, in that not all potential crosses have been tested or reliably documented. Some organisms have even gone extinct. Hybridization is also strictly an *inclusive criterion*, as not even all related animals can produce offspring together (i.e., they have lost the ability to reproduce with certain others of their kind).

The cognitum approach estimates animal kinds using the human senses of perception. This method assumes that animal kinds have maintained their core distinctiveness even as they have diversified over time (*overall* design is equated with common ancestry). Presently, extinct animals are most often classified using this approach. For example, woolly mammoths are extinct, and there are no hybrid data connecting them with elephants. However, their extreme similarity to elephants has resulted in their placement in the elephant kind.

In statistical analyses, continuities and discontinuities of animals are identified by comparing physical traits using statistical tests called baraminic distance correlation (BDC). Like the cognitum approach, this method assumes that the physical similarities and dissimilarities identified in the tests are reliable indictors of relatedness (*specific* designs or differences equate with common ancestry). It also assumes that the traits selected for comparison are baraminologically significant.

What are some safeguards against underestimating the number of Ark animals?

The Ark Encounter researchers put several safeguards in place to avoid underestimating the number of animals on the Ark. These include a tendency to "split" rather than "lump" animal groups. Also, all "clean" and all flying creatures—not just "clean" ones—were multiplied by fourteen instead of seven animals.

What are splitting and lumping?

Estimating the number of animals on the Ark depends upon several factors. Near the top of that list is the decision to split or lump the animals that may or may not be related as a kind.

Coyotes, wolves, dingoes, and domestic dogs can generally interbreed. Thus, they can be lumped into the same kind. So Noah just needed two members of the dog kind on the Ark.

On the other hand, there are approximately two dozen known families of bats, living and extinct. Based on anatomy and other features, many of these families probably belong to the same kind (e.g., if we used the cognitum criteria). In fact, it is possible that every bat belongs to the same kind. However, since breeding studies have not yet confirmed this idea, the Ark Encounter researchers split the bats into their various families. So instead of including as few as 14 bats on the Ark, the information depicts over 300 of them (14 from each family). In keeping with the worst-case approach to estimating the number of animals on the Ark, the animals were split into separate kinds whenever the data was insufficient to support lumping them into a single kind.

Why fourteen instead of seven?

Some Bible translations indicate that Noah was to bring seven of each flying creature and clean animal. Yet other Bibles state that seven pairs of these creatures were on the Ark.

Seven of each kind	Seven pairs of each kind
KJV*	NLT
NKJV	ESV*
NASB*	HCSB
NET*	NRSV
NIV (1984)*	NIV (2011)

* Asterisks indicate that a textual note appears in these Bibles that mentions the possibility of the other view.

The Hebrew text literally reads, "seven seven—a male and his female" (Genesis 7:2). Does this unique phrasing mean seven or fourteen?

In favor of the "seven" view is that Genesis 8:20 states that Noah sacrificed clean animals and birds after the Flood. While it doesn't say that Noah sacrificed just one animal of each clean kind, those who hold to the "seven" view could point to the common "six and one" pattern seen in the Old Testament. For example, God created the world in six days and rested for one (Genesis 1; Exodus 20:11). Perhaps six of each clean animal were for man's use and one was dedicated to the Lord.

In favor of the "seven pairs" view is the text's mention that there would be a male and "his female" for the clean animals. If an odd number were brought to Noah, then plenty of animals did not have a mate. Furthermore, the Hebrew text does not use similar wording with the unclean animals in verse two. That is, readers can know that one pair of unclean animals was in view, but the text does not say "two two, a male and his female"—it just has the word for two.

Since Hebrew language scholars do not agree about this issue, it seems wise to be tentative about which view is accurate. Since a worst-case approach is being used in regard to the animals, these calculations are based on the "seven pairs" position.

What is meant by a "worst-case scenario"?

The Ark Encounter depicts a worst-case approach when estimating the number of animal kinds. Some people believe Noah brought two of every unclean animal and seven of every clean animal. The text seems to indicate that Noah cared for more animals than this (Genesis 7:2–3), particularly when it comes to the clean animals and flying creatures. The Lord may have sent seven pairs of the clean animals and seven pairs of all the flying creatures (not just the clean varieties).

Although this worst-case approach more than doubles the estimated number of animals on the Ark, this model shows that even a high-end estimate of total animals would have fit on board. Obviously, if the Lord sent just seven of each clean animal and seven of just the clean flying creatures, the Ark would have had plenty of space to accommodate this lower total.

How many animal kinds were on the Ark?

Based on initial projections, the Ark Encounter team estimates that there were fewer than 1,400 animal kinds on the Ark. It is anticipated that future research may reduce that number even further.

How many individual animals were on the Ark?

The Ark Encounter team projects that there were fewer than 6,700 animals on board the Ark. The wide discrepancy between the number of Ark kinds and Ark individuals is due to the relatively large number of flying and "clean" kinds—each estimated at 14 animals apiece for this research.

Fossil groups	Kinds (est.)	Per kind	Total animals (est.)
Amphibians	54	2	108
Reptiles	211	Flying 24 x 14 Flightless 187 x 2	710
Non-mammal synapsids	78	2	156
Mammals	314	Clean/flying 13 x 14 Unclean 301 x 2	784
Birds	89	Flying 68 x 14 Flightless 21 x 2	994

Non-fossil groups	Kinds (est.)	Per kind	Total animals (est.)
Amphibians	194	2	388
Reptiles	101	2	202
Mammals	137	Clean/flying 31 x 14 Unclean 106 x 2	646
Birds	195	Flying 190 x 14 Flightless 5 x 2	2,670
Total	1,373		6,658

How big were the Ark animals?

People often wonder how all of the animals could have fit on the Ark, particularly when considering the massive dinosaurs. We see so many illustrations of large creatures packed tightly into a little boat. But this image is inaccurate. Noah's Ark was much larger than it is usually depicted, and many of the animals were probably smaller than shown in popular pictures.

It makes more sense to think that God would have sent to Noah juveniles or smaller varieties within the same kind. Consider the following advantages to bringing juveniles or smaller versions of a creature:

1. They take up less space.

---

2. They eat less.
3. They create less waste.
4. They are often easier to manage.
5. They are generally more durable.
6. In the case of juveniles, they would have more time to reproduce after the Flood.

Indeed, even when the giant dinosaurs and elephant-sized creatures are factored in, the Ark animals were probably much smaller than is frequently assumed. According to Ark Encounter estimates, it is projected only 15 percent of Ark animals would have achieved an average adult mass over 22 pounds (10 kg). This means that the vast majority of Ark animals were smaller than a beagle, with most of those being much smaller. Starting with a mass category of 0.035–0.35 oz. (1–10 g), the animal groups were distributed into eight logarithmically increasing size classes. Amazingly, the size range with the greatest projected number of Ark animals was 0.35–3.5 oz. (10–100 g).

Did the Ark animals hibernate?

One common explanation for how Noah and his family could have cared for so many animals is that the animals hibernated during the voyage. While this would have certainly been convenient for the family, we are not told from Scripture that this was the case. So when the Ark Encounter design team considered food, water, waste management needs, etc., they once again applied their "worst-case scenario" approach and assumed that all the animals were awake and active.

Now, was this actually the case inside the real Ark? Dark, closed-in spaces do tend to induce inactivity in many animals—particularly reptiles, who will often fall into a state of inactivity called torpor. So while many of the Ark animals may have hibernated or been largely inactive for part of the Flood year, it is likely that Noah and his family could not count on this behavior being the norm and would have planned accordingly. After all, God told Noah, "And you shall take for yourself of all food that is eaten, and you shall gather it to yourself; and it shall be food for you and for them" (Genesis 6:21)—that is, the animals. The foregone conclusion is that the animals would be awake to eat these provisions.

Were the animals caged?

Some people assume that the Ark animals were free to roam the Ark, but there are problems with this idea. First, it would not be safe for the animals on a vessel that surely rocked and pitched in the stormy seas. Second, there is no guarantee that all of the Ark's animals were vegetarian. Finally, and most importantly, the Lord told Noah to "make rooms in the ark" (Genesis 6:14). Some Bibles use "nests" instead of "rooms." Essentially, Noah was to make enclosures

The cages displayed at Ark Encounter allow for individual care for the animals while keeping them safely separated.

for the Ark's animals. A cage or pen system was the easiest way to ensure every animal remained safe and received care.

How did they care for creatures with specialized needs?

Many animals today require special care in order for them to survive well in captivity. Hippopotamuses are frequently cited as an example of this, as they have skin that must be kept wet much of the time. Is it unrealistic to believe that Noah and his family could have kept a pair of hippos alive on the Ark?

The Ark had plenty of water, so it's possible that Noah's family developed a system to regularly deliver water to keep the hippos moist. On the other hand, these creatures may not have been as difficult to tend as many people imagine. There are two species of the hippo kind in the world today.

The animal most people think of is the common hippopotamus, but there is also the pygmy hippo. The pygmy hippo is more terrestrial than the common hippo (albeit still semiaquatic), and they are most similar to the fossil hippos found in early post-Flood rock layers. So the Ark's hippos were likely smaller and more terrestrial—and therefore easier to care for—than the large common hippos of today.

How much food would need to be gathered?

Once a number of important data points are logged (e.g., the number of animals, average animal masses and metabolic rates per kind, etc.), a simple formula can be used to estimate the food requirements on the Ark. Based on information collected by Ark Encounter researchers, the minimum bulk food volume needed on the Ark was 17,125 cu. ft. (485 m³) assuming 80% dry matter—that equals over 400 tons (363 tonnes).[4]

Scripture does not record for us if Noah was given all this information, so how could he know how much food to store? It is possible that the family simply loaded the Ark with as much food as it could take, allowing space for other necessities, such as the animal enclosures, working spaces, and living quarters. While constructing the "Half Ark Model" for an exhibit in the Ark Encounter, researchers discovered that everything fit nicely.

What types of food would need to be gathered?

After making everything, the Lord stated that people and animals were to eat vegetation (Genesis 1:29–30). It was not until after the Flood that God permitted man to eat meat (Genesis 9:3). After sin, we cannot be sure when certain animals began to eat meat (it may have been immediate or more gradual), although the fossil record provides strong evidence that carnivory occurred prior to the Flood. If carnivorous activity was prevalent in the pre-Flood world as is implied in Genesis 6:12, it is still possible that the individual animals the Lord sent did not eat meat.

However, if some of the Ark's animals did eat meat, there are several methods of preserving or supplying their food. Meat can be preserved through drying, pickling, salting, or smoking. Certain fish can pack themselves in mud and survive for years without water—these could have been stored on the Ark. Mealworms and other insects can be bred for both carnivores and insectivores.

In any case, most of the animals were vegetarian or could survive as vegetarians for a period of time. To provide food for all of these animals, Noah's family could have grown or purchased vast stores of grains, grasses, seeds, and nuts. Certain vegetables with a long shelf life may have been brought aboard as could dried varieties of some fruits and vegetables.

How could so much food be stored?

Placing food in large silos, bags, or other corruptible containers could have resulted in an unacceptable degree of spoilage and waste. Alternatively, using sealed earthen vessels—perhaps stored in shelving units or bundled together with ropes—would have provided better moisture stability and reduced the likelihood of infestation.

And while Noah's family could have used other storage methods (e.g., barrels and crates), earthenware makes a lot of sense given the simplicity of production and requirements for keeping goods free of contaminants. Strategic placement of food would minimize the effort needed to retrieve and distribute it.

How could the water be collected and stored?

Water has always been at the heart of any civilization. On the Ark it would have been needed for many things as well, such as drinking, cleaning animal stalls, bathing, and washing clothes and dishes.

For this journey, Noah faced a number of challenges related to water management. How much drinking water would be needed? How would they maintain sanitary conditions on board? Would the Ark be able to carry enough water for the duration of the Flood? Could water be collected and used along the way?

Unlike ancient sailors who often relied on staying close to shore or planned stops at islands during long ocean voyages, Noah faced an entire world covered by water. There are numerous examples of early civilizations boiling water or using sand as a filter to acquire safe water. Developing a large-scale method of water treatment for the Ark would have been a monumental feat.

Assuming that Noah did not develop such a process and that the Lord did not miraculously filter the water for them, there are other solutions to ensure the Ark had enough fresh water.

In the history of ships and ocean voyages, water collection using runoff from the sails or through use of barrels on deck has been documented. Neither of these techniques are directly applicable to the Ark, but the basic ideas behind them could be relevant. In order to reduce the occurrence of contamination, water could have been collected beforehand into numerous cisterns, earthen vessels, or other waterproofed containers. In addition to this, using the Ark's roof surface as a massive rainwater collection device would combine elements of sustainability, redundancy, and efficiency—especially if the water could be channeled into overhead cisterns for storage and distribution as needed.

Watering systems

Methods for distributing water in the various areas throughout the Ark—e.g., amphibian containers, small animal cages, large animal enclosures, and human living spaces—may have varied. It would have been unnecessarily laborious and time-consuming for the family members to carry large containers of water around all day. Instead, utilizing a simple system of fixed pipes and spigots would permit easy access to water from the animal pens, living quarters, and other areas.

Bamboo is a practical, natural material for this task, being strong, lightweight, easily cultivated, and resistant to degradation. But we can leave open the option of using more advanced materials as well—recall the pre-Flood world was not primitive.

Aside from the water collection and distribution systems, each animal cage could have been equipped with simple, appropriately sized, vacuum-fed water containers—similar to those still in use today, though possibly crafted as specialized earthen vessels. Such a design would accomplish significant time and labor savings, particularly for the larger animals. Though working in two-person teams is often the most efficient arrangement, utilizing partially automated systems would mean that single tasks would not always require the attention of both individuals. This is crucial since the Ark contained only eight laborers.

Feeding systems

The feeding systems on the Ark would have been much easier to develop than the watering systems. For large animal enclosures, bamboo or wood chutes leading to a food dish could have been filled from an overhead catwalk. External chutes leading to interior food trays could have also been used in the small animal cages, greatly accelerating the feeding process.

Wastewater systems

It is a simple but unpleasant fact of life—both humans and animals produce liquid and solid waste. Without an effective management system for removal of this waste from living areas, people and animals can sicken and eventually die. Put a large number of animals with eight people in a closed environment like the Ark for about a year during the Flood, and it is a huge challenge that had to be addressed before the journey began. It is inevitable that there would have been a solution on board the ship for a number of reasons.

1. The design of the vessel was not meant for either crew or animals to be walking about on the roof of the Ark, at least not while it was afloat. During the Flood event, the only decks that could be walked on safely on a regular basis were interior ones.
2. While there is a door noted for the Ark, it likely could not be opened during transit.
3. There was an opening at the top of the Ark, but nothing hints at this being a site that waste products could be efficiently tossed out of without landing on areas of the roof and causing sanitation problems. More importantly, if Noah's family collected rainwater from the roof for their water supply, as discussed previously, they would not want to pollute it with sewage.
4. The amount of labor it would take to remove the waste using various types of manual labor alone would have been

difficult but manageable. The system solutions for human waste and animal waste could have been completely different, but they may have had a common collection point and labor-reducing method of removal from the ship.

Animal waste

Factoring in the sizes, number, and estimated metabolisms of the projected 6,658 Ark animals, it is likely that the daily solid waste production on the Ark reached a few tons. Human occupant contributions would have been negligible.

The Ark Encounter designs show Noah's family using carts and small wagons to move the solid animal waste. While this sounds like a lot of work, it would have been manageable. Some manual cleaning would be expected even with solutions built into the cage or enclosure designs. The design of the enclosures could have made the waste removal task much simpler. Sloped floors or designs that incorporated slatted floors could have been used—the latter would have permitted waste to slip through and col-

lect below. Large animal enclosures, on the other hand, are typically designed with flat and solid floors, since slotted floors can result in leg or foot injuries.

Concerning liquid waste, collection points funneling into bamboo pipes could have moved urine and excess water away from the enclosures. Each enclosure complex could have been connected to a central waste-water collection tank. While the inclusion of bedding often increases animal comfort, storing and appropriately distributing it takes a lot of space and effort. Thus, it may have been deemed unnecessary for the yearlong stay aboard the Ark.

A hole in the ship?

One significant design feature proposed as a potential component of the Ark is a moonpool. A moonpool is essentially a large cavity running from the bottom of the ship to the upper deck or roof. Even though the moonpool is open to the ocean, the water is confined within its interior, moving up and down like a piston of an engine. The Ark Encounter designers proposed two moonpools in the stern, straddling the keel. One moonpool they designed for ventilation, as the in-and-out movement of the water acts like a massive bellows, circulating fresh air throughout the Ark. The other was designed as an integral part of the waste removal system, exploiting the moonpool's secure access to the waters outside the Ark.

Light source solutions

While it may not receive as much attention as other solutions, lighting surely played a key role in life on the Ark. Whether providing an energy source for growing supplemental plants or making it easier to complete chores in the depths of the ship, it was essential that methods be found for all the lighting needs on the Ark. We are not sure what the "covering" was that Noah opened (Genesis 8:13), but if it was a roof that was translucent or could be drawn back, then this could have allowed light to fill the Ark. Also, oil lamps (or other technologies) could have been used to light the interior. Roof panels could be raised and lowered so that natural light would be utilized on the Ark. Windows are another potential source of natural light.

Is this how they actually did it?

It is easy to let your imagination wander when it comes to the possibilities of how the Ark worked. However, it is always important to come back to what we know from the Scriptures and consider practical solutions that have worked well in the past. The point of the ship was not simply to save eight members of one family—that would have certainly been easier! Noah's task also included the care of all the animals the Lord brought to him.

The possible solutions provided in this chapter really just scratch the surface of what Noah and his family could have designed and built for the real Ark. One thing is for certain, though. We know that in the end, "Thus Noah did; according to all that God commanded him, so he did" (Genesis 6:22). Whichever solutions Noah developed, we can certainly give thanks for the faithfulness of our brilliant ancestor.

1. Laura Welch, ed. *Inside Noah's Ark: Why It Worked* (Green Forest, AR: Master Books, 2016).

2. IUCN 2014. IUCN Red List of Threatened Species. Version 2014.2. iucnredlist.org. Downloaded on 9 November 2016.

3. These last two methods are admittedly subjective and play off of the assumption of common design equating with common ancestry. Even though these methods are utilized, the results are not seen as absolute. There are examples where these methods have failed to be accurate in certain instances. But due to the limited amount of hybridization data, we are left with no other choice.

4. Noah's family and the animals were on the Ark for about a year. They exited the Ark a year and ten days after the Flood began, but we are not certain what calendar is referenced in Genesis 7–8, so we cannot know how many days were in that year. This calculation is based on a 360-day year. Eleven days were added to account for the additional 10 days into the second year and the first and last days in the Ark.

Mike Belknap holds a bachelor of science degree in biology from East Texas Baptist University. He is assistant content writer for the Attractions Division of Answers in Genesis.

Tim Chaffey holds a master of divinity degree, specializing in apologetics and theology, and a master of theology degree in church history and theology from Liberty University School of Divinity. He is content manager for the Attractions Division of Answers in Genesis. An apologist with a passion for training young people, Tim speaks regularly at the Creation Museum, camps, schools, and churches, and has authored numerous books.

Has Noah's Ark Been Found?

by Tim Chaffey

The discovery of Noah's Ark would be an unparalleled archaeological find. Throughout history, thousands of individuals have searched various mountains for the remains of this wooden structure described in the Bible and in numerous legends from cultures around the world.

Ancient reports speak of the Ark as being readily accessible to certain groups of people, even describing an annual festival that supposedly took place on a mountain slope to commemorate the Ark's landing. Pieces of the Ark were allegedly taken and used as amulets.

In the past century, dozens of individuals have claimed to have located the Ark. Most of these modern searches have focused on Mount Ararat in Eastern Turkey. While some of these explorers claimed to have found the Ark or its remains, others are a little more cautious. They call attention to an assortment of evidence that seems to support their beliefs, such as pieces of wood found high on the mountain, as well as aerial and satellite images that show an "Ark-like" structure.

Mt. Ararat, which is traditionally thought to be the landing place of the Ark, is located in eastern Turkey near the border with Armenia and Iran.

Despite so many supposed sightings and evidences from Mount Ararat, it seems unlikely that Noah's Ark has been found in recent times. And even though we would be ecstatic if the Ark were discovered, we have reason to doubt that it will be found in the future. Nor would it convince the skeptics who would simply claim it is a replica monument to a mythical boat. Certainly, it is hard to imagine a large wooden structure surviving the elements for more than 4,000 years. Also, if Mount Ararat truly were the landing place, how could the Ark have survived this volcano's numerous eruptions, which continued until 1840?

These factors have not stopped the search for the Ark or the reported sightings of it. This chapter will focus on five of the most popular locations for the Ark's final resting place. Four of the locations are on or very near Mount Ararat, while the other site lies hundreds of miles from this famous peak.

Site one: the Durupinar site

Popularized in the 1980s by Ron Wyatt and others, this "Ark-shaped" formation lies approximately 15 miles from the summit of Mount Ararat. Wyatt claimed to have found numerous artifacts in the vicinity to corroborate his claims. In the past few years, the Durupinar site has again risen to prominence after being promoted on several websites as the real Noah's Ark.

Despite its "Ark-like" appearance and popularity, Christian geologists and archaeologists who would love to find the Ark and who have visited the location have soundly rejected the Durupinar site as nothing more than a geologic formation.[1]

In fact, several similar-looking formations can be found in the region, as a simple "Google Maps" search demonstrates. These formations are caused by mud flowing around eroded outcrops of basalt lava flows.[2]

Often heralded as the remains of Noah's Ark, the Durupinar site is actually just one of many similar-looking geologic formations in this region of Turkey.

Site two: the Ahora Gorge

The Ahora Gorge is an enormous chasm on the northeast side of Mount Ararat. Dropping more than one mile from the peak of the mountain, the Ahora Gorge has been at the forefront of Ark-seeker expeditions for about a century.

Interest in this location was sparked by the claims of George Hagopian. He claimed that when he was a young boy in 1908, his uncle took him up Mount Ararat to the Ahora Gorge area. Hagopian said that they found something that looked like a large ship partially buried by snow and ice. He claimed his uncle stood on a rock pile and lifted him up so that he could walk on the roof.

At least a dozen expeditions have explored the Ahora Gorge since Hagopian reportedly walked on the Ark's roof. However to date, none of these adventurers have been able to find the remains of Noah's Ark at the Ahora Gorge, even

though they have used satellite imagery, and explorers have searched the gorge when the glacier in it has melted back.

It is very tempting to dismiss Hagopian's incredible claims as the imaginations of a young child. Consider the following complications with his story. Hagopian offered conflicting reports of his adventure. Was he eight years old or ten years old at the time? Was it in 1905 or 1908? Also, it is hard to imagine a youngster making this very difficult and dangerous journey without proper training.

Perhaps the greatest problem with claiming this site as the resting place of the Ark is the fact that the Ahora Gorge is on Mount Ararat. Despite popular beliefs, the Bible does not specify that the Ark landed on Mount Ararat. It states that the Ark landed on the "mountains of Ararat" (Genesis 8:4). In other words, the Ark landed in the region of the land of Ararat.

As mentioned above, this dormant volcano last erupted in 1840, and many much larger eruptions occurred during the post-Flood Ice Age. In fact, the Ahora Gorge was largely constructed by an 1840 earthquake and the resultant catastrophic erosion. Yet even though these Ark searchers say the Ark could have slid down after the gorge formed, it still begs the question as to how a wooden structure would have survived being buried by the molten lavas which erupted since the Flood ended. According to geologist Dr. Andrew Snelling, Mount Ararat likely emerged from the waters of the Flood far too late for it to have been the mountain on which the Ark ran aground on the 17th day of the 7th month of Noah's 600th year.

Site three: the Ararat Anomaly

We have already examined two of the popular locations of reported sightings and found them to be problematic. We will now look at another spot that has caught the eye of Ark researchers, known as the Ararat Anomaly.

In 1949, photographs of the northwest side of Mount Ararat were taken by a United States intelligence agency. A large structure can be seen jutting out of the ice and snow near the middle of the photograph below.

This object has captured the imagination of Ark hunters because it resembles a portion of a large ship. Of course, this "anomaly" may simply be a rock outcropping with just the right amount of ice and snow melted away to give the illusion of a boat-shaped object.

A satellite image taken in 2003 has breathed new life into the popularity of the Ararat Anomaly. Presumably taken of the same spot on the mountain, this overhead shot shows an elongated structure that appears to have similar dimensions to Noah's Ark (circled below).

As far as I know, no expedition has explored the site of the Ararat Anomaly, but it would certainly be a stretch to conclude that these pictures are definitive proof of the Ark's remains on Mount Ararat. The object in the images may be nothing more than a natural rock formation. Perhaps that's why Ark searchers have not been inclined to explore this anomaly.

Furthermore, as mentioned in the previous section, finding the Ark on Mount Ararat is highly unlikely.

Site four: Ararat—NAMI Expedition

In April 2010, a team of evangelical Christian explorers claimed to have found evidence of Noah's Ark on Mount Ararat during their expedition there two years earlier, high up a prominent canyon on the south face of the mountain. The team represents Noah's Ark Ministries International (NAMI), which is part of Hong Kong-based Media

Evangelism. This group claims to be a Christian organization committed to developing a Christian media presence to promote the message of Jesus Christ.

This group claimed to have found or were told about seven wooden compartments buried on Mount Ararat, which they believe were part of Noah's Ark. They even produced a video showing team members presumably inside one of these wooden structures.

Although we would be delighted if the Ark had actually been found, this "discovery" is likely a hoax. This is not to accuse NAMI of perpetrating the hoax, but there is a real possibility that they were victims of a fraud enacted by a Kurdish man called Paraşut.

Dr. Randall Price and Dr. Don Patton were the experts invited to be part of the expedition, but they were never permitted to see the site and were soon dropped from the team. They have documented many of the inconsistencies between what was reported and what they found in their research. For example, pictures of an alleged room in the Ark provided by Paraşut show straw, cobwebs, and a feed bowl, each in very good condition. The problem with these images is that Paraşut has claimed that the site is frequently flooded, which was his reason for not taking the expedition there in the summer months. Would a site that endured regular flooding remain in good shape for millennia?

They also interviewed a Kurdish worker who claimed to have been one of several people hired by Paraşut to construct "movie sets" on the mountain. For more details, you can read the full 52-page exposé by Dr. Price and Dr. Patton.[3]

Finally, as mentioned above in the sections about the Ararat Anomaly and the Ahora Gorge, finding the Ark on modern-day Mount Ararat is highly unlikely. This mountain is a dormant volcano, and it likely emerged from the Flood waters far too late for it to have been the mountain on which the Ark landed.

Site five: Ararat—Mount Suleiman

The Bible states that the Ark landed on the "mountains of Ararat" (Genesis 8:4). Many people believe that Mount Ararat in Eastern Turkey is in view here, but the Bible merely places the Ark on a mountain in the region of Ararat, called Urartu in ancient times. As such, it is certainly possible that the Ark landed on a mountain other than Mount Ararat.

A military veteran named Ed Davis claimed to have seen the remains of Noah's Ark during World War II while he was stationed in Iran. Based on his understanding of this report, Bob Cornuke of the BASE Institute led expeditions to Mount Suleiman, also called the Throne of Solomon, in 2005 and 2006 to explore an alternative site for Noah's Ark.

Cornuke provided several details about the site that he believes is a candidate for the remains of Noah's Ark. His team found rocks that were "uncannily beam like in appearance" over 13,000 feet up the mountain, "a worship shrine," and fossilized clams in abundance on the top of an adjoining peak. Cornuke also points to the wide variety of ecosystems in the region and the 1965 rediscovery of the Caspian horse, believed by some to be the most ancient variety of domestic horse.[4]

Despite these assertions, there are multiple problems with the notion that the Ark came to rest on Mount Suleiman. For example, the beam-like rocks are likely a geological formation, the eroded edge of upended, finely bedded rock layers, according to geologists who have only been able to examine pictures. Also, it is improbable that Ed Davis' reported sighting took place on Mount Suleiman. But the biggest problem is that Mount Suleiman lies 250 miles east of the farthest-known reaches of the ancient Urartu region. As such, this mountain doesn't match the biblical description that the Ark came to rest on the mountains of Ararat (Genesis 8:4).

Conclusion

Expeditions will continue to search for the Ark. While it probably has not survived the elements for thousands of years, we can be confident that it really did exist because God's Word has infallibly recorded the account of the Flood. Answers in Genesis' Ark Encounter themed attraction in Williamstown, Kentucky shows the feasibility of this famous vessel and uses the biblical account of Noah, the Ark, and the Flood to share the gospel of Jesus Christ.

---

1. See John Morris, "That Boat Shaped Rock . . . Is It Noah's Ark?," Answers in Genesis, September 1, 1990, answersingenesis.org/creationism/arguments-to-avoid/that-boat-shaped-rock-is-it-noahs-ark/ and Rick Lanser, "Noah's Ark Update," Associates for Biblical Research, September 26, 2008, biblearchaeology.org/post/2008/09/26/Noahs-Ark-Update.aspx#Article.

2. For a geologist's detailed critique of the claims and artifacts that supposedly support this place as Noah's Ark, please read Dr. Andrew Snelling's exposé of Ron Wyatt's claims at answersingenesis.org/creationism/arguments-to-avoid/special-report-amazing-ark-expose/.

3. See worldofthebible.com/wp-content/uploads/2017/05/Fall2010.pdf.

4. Each of these claims is mentioned in an article from the BASE Institute. See baseinstitute.org/pages/noahs_ark/17.

Noah the Evangelist

by Paul F. Taylor and Gary Vaterlaus

Christians have gleaned many valuable lessons from Noah and the Ark. But one fact is often overlooked. He was the first evangelist mentioned in the Bible. Are there any lessons his life can teach us about how to present the gospel? Absolutely!

For one, Noah faced the same circumstances that Christians face today.

> As the days of Noah were, so also will the coming of the Son of Man be. For as in the days before the flood, they were eating and drinking, marrying and giving in marriage, until the day that Noah entered the ark, and did not know until the flood came and took them all away, so also will the coming of the Son of Man be. (Matthew 24:36–39)

A certain future

The analogy is very instructive. Just as most people today do not believe Jesus is coming back at all, let alone soon, the people of Noah's day did not know when the Flood was going to happen. However, they were informed that there was indeed going to be a Flood. Their information came from many sources:

1. from the fact that Noah was actually building an Ark.

2. from the warning of God's Spirit (Genesis 6:3 says, "And the Lord said, 'My Spirit shall not strive with man forever, for he is indeed flesh; yet his days shall be one hundred and twenty years.'").

3. quite likely, from the words of Noah himself.

Like people today, almost certainly the people of Noah's day were busy enjoying the pleasures of life and did not believe or care that judgment was coming.

During the decades of mankind's last days, Noah was working on the Ark. As it grew, it must have been a potent symbol to those living nearby. One can imagine that Noah was often asked about his construction project. Indeed, it is likely that he was mocked for such an enterprise.

A silent preacher and his faith

In 2 Peter 2:5, Noah is described as a "preacher of righteousness." In what way was he a preacher? The Greek word *kerux* (κηρυξ) refers to a herald, or "one who announces." Even when he wasn't saying anything, his labor on the Ark would have been his witness. However, some Jewish scholars maintain that Noah did indeed leave some words, too. John Gill, in chapter 22 of the *Pirke R. Eliezer*, quotes Noah's words according to Jewish tradition: "Be ye turned from your evil ways and works, lest the waters of the flood come upon you, and cut off all the seed of the children of men."

The tradition shows Noah giving both a warning and a means of salvation. If this extrabiblical source has any truth in it, then Noah is asking for people to repent, which would certainly fit with his own source of salvation through Christ. Noah was not saved because of his righteousness—at least not in a worldly sense. Hebrews 11 tells us from where Noah's righteousness came. The Greek word is *dikaiosune* (δικαιοσύνη), which refers to a form of righteousness that is unattainable by law or by merit.

Hebrews 11:7 says, "By faith Noah, being divinely warned of things not yet seen, moved with godly fear, prepared an ark for the saving of his household, by which he condemned the world and became heir of the righteousness which is according to faith."

This sort of righteousness is found only by faith. The Apostle Paul says elsewhere, "For by grace you have been saved through faith, and that not of yourselves; it is the gift of God, not of works, lest anyone should boast" (Ephesians 2:8–9).

This is exactly how Noah was saved. His righteousness was unattainable; so it could only come by God's grace, through faith. Genesis 6:8 tells us that "Noah found grace in the eyes of the Lord." Noah's salvation, like ours, was by grace. He could not do anything to attain righteousness for himself.

An available safety

In His instructions for building the Ark, God told Noah to "set the door of the Ark in its side" (Genesis 6:16). The Ark had only one door to pass through to escape God's terrible judgment. By faith, Noah and his family entered the Ark. Once they were all inside, the Lord shut them in (Genesis 7:16).

What is significant about God shutting the door of the Ark? It provides a wonderful demonstration of the twin truths of man's responsibility and God's sovereignty that we see throughout Scripture.

When the door to the Ark was shut, there was room for many more people. All they had to do was repent and turn to God. In the same way, salvation is available to "whoever calls on the name of the Lord" (Romans 10:13). Notice that the eight occupants of the Ark entered by a door—and there was only one door—which was not closed by Noah, but by God—"the Lord shut him in" (Genesis 7:16). Jesus said, "I am the door. If anyone enters by Me, he will be saved" (John 10:9). The Ark pictures salvation in Jesus Christ, our "Ark" of salvation.

The willing Savior

Noah's Flood teaches us two things about the attitude of God toward us.

He is angry with sin and will punish it one day.

He loves us and sends us a way of salvation, if we will only repent and turn to Him.

Jesus is our Ark of Salvation today. Just as Noah was saved by grace through faith from the destruction of the Flood, we can be saved by grace through faith in Jesus, when we repent and turn to Him.

The Bible makes it clear that we are "dead in trespasses and sins" (Ephesians 2:1). Nothing we can do can save us from our sin and its consequence of eternal separation from God. But the Bible also tells us that if we confess with our mouth the Lord Jesus and believe in our heart that God has raised Him from the dead, we will be saved (Romans 10:9). It is "by grace you have been saved through faith, and that not of yourselves; it is the gift of God" (Ephesians 2:8). Nothing we can do will save us from our sin—salvation is all of God. Yet our responsibility is to go through the doorway (Jesus), and God will save us.

All Christians, just as Noah, have a responsibility to share the message of salvation with a world that is perishing. The lessons from the account of Noah are a great reminder of that truth.

Paul F. Taylor graduated with his BSc in chemistry from Nottingham University and his masters in science education from Cardiff University. Paul taught science for 17 years in a state school and served as a senior speaker for Answers in Genesis–UK.

Gary Vaterlaus earned his undergraduate and master's degrees in science education from Oregon State University. He also studied at Western Conservative Baptist Seminary. He is director of curriculum development for Answers in Genesis–US.

Taking Back the Rainbow

by Ken Ham

From my childhood days as a lad in Australia to my travels today as a speaker with Answers in Genesis, I've seen scores—probably hundreds—of these amazing multicolored arches. Whether seen from the back seat of the family station wagon as it bounced down a dirt road in rural Queensland, or the window seat of a jetliner flying over a storm below, these beautiful bows remind me of my parents' teaching of what the Bible says about God's purpose in giving us the rainbow.

Twisted truth

Rainbows have come to be identified as symbolic of three basic concepts:

Promises—Genesis 9 records God's promise to Noah that He would never again destroy all flesh with a global flood.

Creation—Folklore and regional legends position the rainbow a bit differently. For example, Australian Aborigine and American Indian legends link it to creation events, and the Chinese have a legend concerning the rainbow and the creation of their first emperor Fohi.

Bridges—The rainbow has also been used to represent a bridge from earth (from humans) to a brighter, happier place. For instance, Judy Garland's "Somewhere Over the Rainbow" represents connecting to a happier place. The New Age religious movement also uses the rainbow as a bridge.

The rainbow has been used as a sign of a new era and a symbol of peace, love, and freedom. Sadly, the colors of the rainbow are even used on a flag for the gay and lesbian movement.

A biblical covenant of grace

However, the true meaning of the rainbow is revealed in Genesis 9:12–15:

> This is the sign of the covenant which I make between Me and you, and every living creature that is with you, for perpetual generations: I set My rainbow in the cloud, and it shall be for the sign of the covenant between Me and the earth. It shall be, when I bring a cloud over the earth, that the rainbow shall be seen in the cloud; and I will remember My covenant which is between Me and you and every living creature of all flesh; the waters shall never again become a flood to destroy all flesh.

First, the covenant of the rainbow is between God and man and the animal kinds that were with Noah on the Ark: a promise that there would never be such an event again that would destroy all flesh on the land. As there have been many local floods since that time, this is obviously a promise there would never be another global flood to destroy all flesh.

The Bible states clearly that there will be a future, global judgment, but next time by fire, not water (2 Peter 3:10). Some commentators even suggest that the watery colors of the rainbow (the blue end of the spectrum) remind us of the destruction by water, and the fiery colors (the red end of the spectrum) of the coming destruction by fire.

Secondly, the rainbow is a covenant of grace. It is actually a symbol of Christ Himself.

When the secular world hears the account of Noah's global Flood, they often accuse God of being an ogre for bringing this terrible judgment on people. However, the God of the Bible is a God of infinite mercy and grace.

God told Noah to build an Ark to save representative land animal kinds and Noah's family. However, this Ark was much larger than needed for just these animals and this family. Just as Noah and his family had to go through the door to be saved, so others could have gone through that door to be saved. In fact, after the Ark was loaded, it stood for seven more days before God Himself shut the door—seven more days of grace. And I have no doubt that Noah preached from the doorway, imploring people to come in and be saved. Noah's Ark is actually a picture of salvation in Christ, as He is the door through which we need to go to be saved for eternity (John 10:9).

All need to be reminded that we sinned in Adam—we committed high treason against the God of creation. God is holy and pure—completely without sin. A holy God has to judge sin, but in His judgment, He also shows infinite mercy. When God judged sin with death in Genesis 3:19, He also promised a Savior (Genesis 3:15). God Himself, in the person of the second member of the Trinity, the Lord Jesus Christ, stepped into history, fully human and fully God, to be a man so He could pay the penalty for our sin. Through the shedding of His blood, He offers the free gift of salvation to all who will believe.

The Bible reveals to us that the rainbow is a symbol of Christ in Ezekiel 1:26–28. In Revelation 4:2–3, John saw Christ clothed with a cloud and a rainbow on His head.

As Bible scholar John Gill states concerning the rainbow, "As it has in it a variety of beautiful colors, it may represent Christ, who is full of grace and truth, and fairer than the children of men; and may be considered as a symbol of peace and reconciliation by him, whom God looks unto, and remembers the covenant of his grace he has made with him and his chosen ones in him; and who is the rainbow round about the throne of God, and the way of access unto it."[1]

The next time you see a rainbow, remember that God judges sin. But He is also merciful, and He made a covenant of grace with Noah and the animals—He will never again judge with a worldwide Flood.

A reminder for all of us

So the next time you see a rainbow, remember that God judges sin. He judged with a global flood at the time of Noah. But He is merciful, and He made a covenant of grace with Noah and the animals that He would never again judge with a worldwide Flood. Not only that, but the rainbow, as a symbol of Christ, reminds us that He is the mediator between man and God and that those who receive the free gift of salvation are presented faultless before their Creator.

God declares those redeemed who have trusted in Christ. They are clothed in the righteousness of His Son. For the redeemed, the wrath of God toward sin was satisfied on the Cross—paid in full by the shed blood of His sinless Son.

And as John Gill puts it, "Though it is a bow, yet without arrows, and is not turned downwards towards the earth, but upwards towards heaven, and so is a token of mercy and kindness, and not of wrath and anger."[1]

I'm so thankful for a mum and dad who used what opportunities they had to instill in my siblings and me the truths of Scripture. Yes, we need to take the meaning of the rainbow back, and use it to tell the world of the mercy and kindness of our Creator and Savior, just like my mum and dad told me.

---

1. *John Gill's Exposition of the Entire Bible*, adapted from Online Bible by Larry Pierce.

The Ark and the Gospel

As we ponder the scriptural account of Noah and the Ark, we cannot help but recognize God's judgment as the reason for the Flood. Many will take exception to the idea of a loving God wiping out the entire population of the earth, except for eight people. But that is exactly what is revealed in God's own words recorded by the pen of Moses. In Genesis 6:5–7 we read:

> Then the LORD saw that the wickedness of man was great in the earth, and that every intent of the thoughts of his heart was only evil continually. And the LORD was sorry that He had made man on the earth, and He was grieved in His heart. So the LORD said, "I will destroy man whom I have created from the face of the earth, both man and beast, creeping thing and birds of the air, for I am sorry that I have made them."

But the sin of mankind did not start here—it had escalated to this point. Adam and Eve chose to rebel against God's command in the Garden of Eden. They willfully ate of the forbidden fruit and brought sin into the human race. This sin multiplied to the point that God judged the entire earth. God offered salvation from the judgment aboard the Ark. All a person had to do was to recognize the position that his sins had put him in and humbly accept the open door of the Ark.

This account offers a parallel to our condition as humans today. God promised that He would never again judge the sin of mankind with a global flood. But another kind of judgment day is coming for all mankind.

Like Adam and Eve, each person on the earth has violated God's standard of righteousness—perfect obedience to His will. If you doubt your guilt before God, stop and think about the Ten Commandments as a summary of God's moral Law. Has God always been first in your life (Exodus 20:3–6)? Have you always obeyed and honored your parents (Exodus 20:12)? Have you ever stolen anything or told a lie (Exodus 20:15–16)? Jesus said that even if you look with lust you are guilty of committing adultery (Matthew 5:28). God judges not only our outward actions, but the intents of our heart. If we are honest, we will admit that we have broken His law uncountable times and we can never live up to His holy standard. Just as Paul said in Romans 3:23, "all have sinned and fall short of the glory of God."

God's punishment for the first sin involved both physical death and spiritual separation from God. Likewise, we die today as a penalty of sin. After we die physically, we will face God as our Judge, and He will judge our thoughts and words and deeds (Hebrews 9:27). This is the bad news; so now for the good news.

Just as God offered salvation from the judgment of the Flood by way of the single door of the Ark, He also offers salvation from the judgment to come through another "door." In John 10:9 Jesus referred to himself as "the door" and said, "If anyone enters by Me, he will be saved." So how does Jesus provide this offer of salvation?

After Adam and Eve had sinned, God killed animals and covered their shame with skins. This was the foreshadowing of the sacrificial system that was instituted through Moses to ceremonially cover over the sins of those who offered animal sacrifices in the Tabernacle and the Temple. But those sacrifices were just another picture of the ultimate sacrifice that God would provide to actually give people forgiveness of sin and a restored relationship with Him. He promised that Savior (Seed) to redeem the world way back in the Garden of Eden (Genesis 3:15) and then many times again by the Jewish prophets through the centuries.

Because the smallest sin is an infinitely offensive act against a perfectly holy God, the justice of God's judgment on sin can only be satisfied by a perfect sacrifice. That sacrifice came as God stepped into history in the person of Jesus Christ.

Jesus came to the earth, lived a perfectly holy life free of sin, and was then offered as the sacrificial "Lamb of God who takes away the sin of the world" (John 1:29). When Christ died on the Cross, the judgment for sin was poured out on Him. He drank the cup of wrath that was prepared for sinners like you and I. In his death, He is a substitute who bears our penalty. Since God's wrath is satisfied in Christ's perfect obedience and death, we no longer have to bear that penalty. This offer of salvation is extended to all men—but not all men will receive the gift (John 3:16–21). Death has now been defeated through the resurrection of Jesus Christ and eternal life is made available.

In order to receive the offer of forgiveness and eternal life, the good news of the gospel, God commands us to repent of our sins and place our faith in Christ. As Paul traveled on his missionary journeys he preached the need for "repentance toward God and faith toward our Lord Jesus Christ" (Acts 20:21). If you will humble yourself before God and place your faith in the life, death, and resurrection of Jesus Christ (1 Corinthians 15:3–4) you too will pass from death into life.

Just as God extended grace to Noah (Genesis 6:8), grace has also been extended to us in Christ's substitutionary death on the Cross. Salvation is a free gift that cannot be earned:

> For by grace you have been saved through faith, and that not of yourselves; it is the gift of God, not of works, lest anyone should boast. (Ephesians 2:8–9)

Have you received that gift?